Supporting People with Learning Disabilities and Dementia

A self-study guide for support staff (based on the *Supporting Derek* film and guide)

Karen Watchman, Heather Wilkinson and Philly Hare

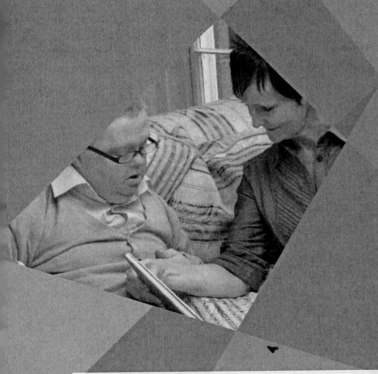

Supporting People with Learning Disabilities and Dementia

A self-study guide for support staff (based on the *Supporting Derek* film and guide)

© Pavilion Publishing and Media Ltd

The authors have asserted their rights in accordance with the Copyright, Designs and Patents Act (1988) to be identified as the authors of this work.

Published by:
Pavilion Publishing and Media Ltd
Blue Sky Offices
Cecil Pashley Way
Shoreham by Sea
West Sussex
BN43 5FF
Tel: 01273 434 943
Email: info@pavpub.com

Published 2018 and 2019

All rights reserved. No part of this publication may be reproduced, stored in a retrieval system, or transmitted in any form or by any means, electronic, mechanical, photocopying, recording or otherwise, without prior permission in writing of the publisher and the copyright owners.

A catalogue record for this book is available from the British Library.

ISBN: 978-1-912755-07-3

Pavilion Publishing and Media is a leading publisher of books, training materials and digital content in mental health, social care and allied fields. Pavilion and its imprints offer must-have knowledge and innovative learning solutions underpinned by sound research and professional values.

Authors: Heather Wilkinson, Karen Watchman and Philly Hare
Production editor: Ruth Chalmers, Pavilion Publishing and Media Ltd.
Cover design: Phil Morash, Pavilion Publishing and Media Ltd.
Page layout and typesetting: Emma Dawe, Pavilion Publishing and Media Ltd.
Printing: Ashford Press

Contents

Acknowledgements 1

About the authors 3

Introduction 5

Chapter 1: Understanding learning disability and dementia 9

Chapter 2: Understanding behaviour 27

Chapter 3: Environment 33

Chapter 4: Responding to pain 45

Chapter 5: Effective communication 51

Chapter 6: Meaningful activities 57

Chapter 7: When a friend has dementia 67

Chapter 8: Eating and drinking 73

Chapter 9: Night-time care 79

Chapter 10: Advanced dementia 85

Additional resources 91

Acknowledgements

We are very grateful to the following groups and individuals who provided feedback and suggestions for this self-study guide:

ENABLE Cuppa Club, Moray; Jeff Gable; Macintyre 'Keep Going, Don't Stop' group, Chesterfield; Nicola Payne, MacIntyre; Home Farm Trust; Dr Hannah Crawford, Tees, Esk and Wear Valleys NHS Foundation Trust; Dr Ken Macmahon, University of Edinburgh; Christine Towers, Together Matters; Hazel Ratcliffe, Ratcliffe Consultancy.

We are delighted to have the support of MacIntyre in the production of this guide.

Thanks also to the original advisory group for the resource *Supporting Derek* published by the Joseph Rowntree Foundation in 2010:

Noelle Blackman, Director, RESPOND; Jan Collis, Lead Inspector, Commission for Social Care Inspection; Peter Cox, Independent Consultant; Karen Dodd, Associate Director for Specialist Therapies – Learning Disabilities and Older People's Mental Health Services, Surrey and Borders Partnership NHS Foundation Trust; Val Ellis, Dementia Specialist Nurse, Joseph Rowntree Housing Trust; Peggy Fray, Independent Consultant; Philly Hare, Programme Manager, Joseph Rowntree Foundation; Diana Kerr, Author; Lou Marsden, Training Officer, Down's Syndrome Association; Henry Simmons, Chief Executive, Alzheimer Scotland; Jen Summers, Publications Manager, Joseph Rowntree Foundation; Christine Towers, Research and Service Development Manager, Foundation for People with Learning Disabilities; Cally Ward, Valuing People Support Team – Family Carers; Kate Wilkinson, Publications Manager, Joseph Rowntree Foundation.

The *Supporting Derek* short film was developed collaboratively with actors Derek, Peter and Theresa from Guyz n Dollz drama group, Support for Ordinary Living (SOL), Motherwell, Scotland. Thanks also to John Phillips and Michael Bernstein, Growing Older with Learning Disabilities (GOLD) group, London for video contributions.

The authors worked collaboratively with a number of other organisations to produce the film. Our thanks go to:

Adult Services, Joseph Rowntree Housing Trust, York; NHS Oldham; Oldham Council; Pennine Care NHS Foundation, Tees, Wear and Esk Valleys NHS Foundation Trusts.

Acknowledgements

The *Supporting Derek* film was directed and produced by Nine Lives Media.

Audit checklists for inside and outside public spaces was reproduced with permission from the University of Edinburgh, Innovations in Dementia and HammondCare Dementia Centre.

About the authors

Dr Karen Watchman has over twenty years' experience in both practice and academic settings working collaboratively with individuals ageing with a learning disability who are affected by dementia. She develops and delivers national and international learning disability and dementia training and education programmes. She leads research into learning disability and dementia at the University of Stirling, Scotland.

Professor Heather Wilkinson has extensive research experience in the field of ageing and learning disability and in the field of dementia. She is Director of the Edinburgh Centre for Research in the Experience of Dementia (E-CRED), University of Edinburgh, Scotland. Her work at ECRED focuses on increasing the involvement of people with dementia in the coproduction of research and impact. She has projects exploring the emotional impact of dementia; the role of dementia activists; dementia signage and design; and collaborations with people with dementia in Japan.

Philly Hare is a Director of the UK-wide social enterprise Innovations in Dementia, and an Exchange Fellow at E-CRED. Her main interest is in enabling people with dementia to have a voice. In her previous role with Joseph Rowntree Foundation, Philly commissioned the first edition of 'Supporting Derek'.

Introduction

As people who have a learning disability grow older, we need to ensure that support and services are geared towards meeting their changing physical and mental health needs. This self-study guide is designed to maintain and improve your skills in supporting people with a learning disability and dementia. You can work through the guide, section by section, completing the activities as you go. The activities will help you to apply your knowledge, while the practice activities will help you to relate that knowledge to working with the individuals you support.

The first edition of this resource, *Supporting Derek*, provided introductory information and suggested activities. This revised self-study guide has been written to benefit staff or volunteers who may find it difficult to attend formal training. The topics and associated content reflect new learning, particularly around talking to people with a learning disability about dementia and future planning.

Since *Supporting Derek* was originally published in 2010, we have seen an increase in research that includes people who have a learning disability and dementia and we are learning more about preferences and choices of individuals who have a diagnosis. This is reflected in the new edition, with a particular emphasis on what this means for practice.

Experience from our own research and training delivery in the UK and internationally has been incorporated and the associated training pack has been piloted with staff teams at different stages of supporting people with a learning disability and dementia, and with peers of people who have a learning disability and dementia.

The original *Supporting Derek* resource has always been recognised as a leader in the field and it is used around the world. We see this update as the next step in supporting staff to take a consistent and informed approach to working with people with learning disabilities and dementia.

Who is this guide for?

This self-study guide is aimed at health and social care practitioners and carers who support:

- people who have a learning disability and dementia
- people who have a learning disability and are at risk of developing dementia in the future
- people who have a learning disability who live or work alongside people who have dementia.

Your work or volunteering may be in any health or social care setting such as a:

- residential setting
- individuals' home (living alone, with family or with friends)
- hospital or allied health facility
- supported housing facility
- respite facility
- community or day care setting
- support group, for example self-advocacy, peer support or campaigning group.

This guide can be used for your continuing professional development. If you are a manager, you might like to ask your staff members or students to work through it section-by-section, completing the activities each contains. Their responses can be discussed as part of on-going reflection and supervision or discussed at a staff handover meeting. The guide can help staff to prepare for quality checks and inspections and can contribute towards meeting national care standards.

There is also a copy of this guide in the *Supporting People with Learning Disabilities and Dementia* training pack, included as background for those facilitating training programmes.

Although not specifically written for family carers, the guide will provide vital information and practical advice.

What does this guide aim to achieve?

The main objective of this guide is to promote holistic support that will maintain the abilities of the person with a learning disability and dementia and provide services that meet their individual needs. It is important that people with a learning disability and dementia:

- have choice and control over the support and services they receive, now and in the future
- maintain meaningful and supportive relationships with family, friends and the wider community
- remain in their own accommodation, if appropriate and desired.

How the guide is structured

Each section in this self-study guide is structured around one of ten topic areas, ranging from background information about learning disability and dementia to end-of-life planning. Each topic area will prompt thinking about practice and development of skills, promoting changes to support which are focused around each individual, rather than expecting the person to fit the service.

Tools are included as part of each topic. They may be copied as handouts, or used as part of staff discussions. Some can also be displayed or made available in a designated staff area for staff to read.

Supporting Derek is a short two-part film featuring actors with a learning disability which can be accessed from: https://www.pavpub.com/supporting-people-with-learning-disabilities-and-dementia-self-study-resources/. This will provide practical examples of some of the issues discussed in this guide and is an essential resource when completing some of the activities.

Suggested further reading is provided for anyone wishing to find out more about issues relating to learning disability and dementia. Please note that websites may change in the future and inclusion in this guide does not imply recommendation.

Terms used

Throughout this pack the term 'dementia' is used to describe a range of conditions that affect the brain. This includes Alzheimer's disease, vascular dementia, Lewy body dementia, frontal lobe dementia and others. Although the generic term 'dementia' is used throughout the training guide, it must be remembered that each person will have a specific type of dementia or may have more than one form of dementia at the same time.

The term 'learning disability' is used throughout, reflecting typical UK terminology, although intellectual disability is commonly used elsewhere. 'Learning disability' is an umbrella term that describes a number of conditions that are present from childhood which affect development. Examples of a learning disability include autism, Fragile-X syndrome, Down's syndrome, Angelman syndrome, Rett syndrome and Prader-Willi syndrome.

Definitions and meanings of 'learning disability' and 'dementia' are discussed further in Chapter 1.

Chapter 1: Understanding learning disability and dementia

Chapter aim: to understand and respond to signs of dementia in people with a learning disability.

As people who have a learning disability grow older, we need to ensure that support and services can meet their changing needs. This chapter provides information about dementia and learning disability and expands on the following links between the two:

- People with learning disabilities now enjoy an increased life expectancy. As individuals age, we continue to learn more about the conditions to which they are susceptible. One of these conditions is dementia.

- Anyone with a learning disability may get a form of dementia, but people with Down's syndrome can be particularly vulnerable at an earlier age.

- Approximately one in three people with Down's syndrome will develop dementia in their 50s. For people who live into their 60s, this figure may increase to at least two in three.

- People with a learning disability other than Down's syndrome may develop dementia on average approximately ten years earlier than those without any form of learning disability. However, the risk is not as high as for people with Down's syndrome.

What is dementia?

- 'Dementia' is an umbrella term that describes a number of conditions of the brain; there is not just one condition called dementia (see Figure 1).

- Dementia is progressive and terminal.

- Common types of dementia include Alzheimer's disease, Lewy Body dementia, Pick's disease, vascular (multi-infarct) dementia and frontal lobe dementia.

- Each type of dementia affects the person in a different way.

- There is no cure for dementia. Medication such as Aricept (Donepezil) may help in the early stages, although it may cause side effects.
- Early indicators of dementia may not always be obvious changes in memory. There might be changes in daily living skills, in behavior or personality, struggling to find the right word to use, or changes in sight and hearing.

Figure 1: Dementia: the umbrella term

What is a learning disability?

- 'Learning disability' is another umbrella term that describes a number of conditions that are present from childhood and affect development.
- People with a learning disability, like all of us, have their own personality, background and potential, and should be seen, first and foremost, as individuals.
- A learning disability is not an illness or a disease.
- Learning disabilities include autism, Fragile-X syndrome, Down's syndrome, Angelman's syndrome, Rett syndrome, Prader-Willi syndrome and others that are non-specific.

- Having a learning disability can result in a reduced ability to understand new information.
- Having a learning disability can result in a reduced ability to cope independently.
- Additional support is usually needed; the amount will vary between individuals or as health needs change.
- Different behaviours, forms of communication and characteristics are associated with different types of learning disability.

Dementia and learning disability

While many of the issues faced by people with dementia in the general population are the same for people with a learning disability, there are some additional points that those providing support need to be aware of:

- Diagnosis of dementia is harder, and can take longer, due to the communication difficulties that people may already have. This can lead to the belief that dementia progresses more quickly, whereas the delay in diagnosis is often a contributory factor.
- It is often assumed that the only type of dementia that people with Down's syndrome will get is Alzheimer's disease. Although people with Down's syndrome are most vulnerable to Alzheimer's disease, this does not mean that they do not develop other types of dementia as well, such as Lewy body dementia and frontal lobe dementia or a combination of more than one type. Indeed, there may be a higher occurrence of frontal lobe dementia in people with Down's syndrome than previously thought.
- People with a learning disability other than Down's syndrome can live with dementia for as many years as people without a learning disability. For people with Down's syndrome though, the progression to end stages and death is usually much quicker. This may in part be due to delay in diagnosis.
- While many people without a learning disability are supported by their partners or adult children, this is less common for people with a learning disability as they are more often single.
- As parents may no longer be alive, siblings, friends, partners and previous carers play an important role in giving support, personal history and background information.

Identifying dementia in people with a learning disability

Complexities around understanding how dementia is experienced by people with a learning disability, and lack of awareness of dementia as a possible diagnosis, mean that people with a learning disability are even less likely to receive a timely diagnosis than people in the population generally.

A lack of clear information about who to refer the person to can often delay a diagnosis. Barriers to consistent attendance at appointments, access to psychological assessment and willingness to undergo neuroimaging and phlebotomy can be barriers to diagnosis. A lack of a baseline assessment from which to monitor change can also delay a diagnosis. Learning disability psychiatrists, where available, and psychologists or GPs, can help with screening or assessment, as can allied health professionals and community learning disability nurses. Ideally, the same person/team will repeat any screening or assessment, using the same tool for consistency.

Everyone who knows the person can and should be involved in monitoring and identifying changes. Once there is a suspicion that someone may have dementia, it is essential that a referral is made as soon as possible.

Early signs of dementia in people with a learning disability

It is essential to pick up as early as possible any changes that may indicate that the person has dementia. It is important that dementia be understood as more than just loss of memory.

The most common changes to look out for are:

- deterioration in daily living skills
- increased inactivity
- loss of interest in previously enjoyed activities
- reduced communication
- new or increased confusion and/or disorientation
- changes in sleep pattern

- difficulty in perceiving depth, such as going up or down stairs or a pavement/roadside.
- increased walking about without a clear reason
- changes to sight or hearing.

Remember, if a person has always shown such traits this is not indicative of dementia unless there is a change to the typical behaviour pattern.

Seizures can be seen in most people with Down's syndrome around two to three years after the onset of dementia, but often a referral is made only when this major and obvious change occurs. Seizures are also seen in some people with a learning disability other than Down's syndrome by the end stage of dementia. These seizures are not necessarily big events and may be in the form of myoclonic jerks (sudden muscle contractions) or even just 'absences' (lapses in awareness, sometimes staring into space).

Ruling out other possibilities

Misdiagnosis of dementia can occur because the signs are the same as those for a number of treatable conditions. For example, people with depression can be withdrawn, less active, have problems with sleep and lose interest in previous pursuits. They may also stop engaging in their usual activities of daily living. All these signs can also indicate dementia. A person can also develop an acute confusional state and, again, we may associate this with dementia, but many other things can also be the cause, including:

- lack of sleep
- infection, particularly a urinary tract infection (UTI)
- the effects of certain medications or mixing medications – regular medication reviews should take place, especially for long-term use of antipsychotic medication
- thyroid problems
- untreated pain
- dehydration
- constipation
- poorly managed diabetes
- malnutrition and/or poor diet

...ies

...d/or visual impairment

...ons.

A reaction to bereavement or other recent changes can also bring about similar signs which the person may not be able to put into words. Additionally, women with Down's syndrome may experience symptoms linked to the menopause, which could be mistaken for dementia, not least because the age of onset may be similar.

Assessment and diagnosis

Baseline assessment

Whilst population screening for dementia is not generally recommended, this differs for people with Down's syndrome. A baseline assessment of abilities before the onset of dementia is important, as it offers a starting point from which significant and lasting change can be noted and measured. It is recommended that baseline assessments take place for all people with Down's syndrome from the age of 30, repeated every two years up to the age of 50 and every year after that. Health screening clinics for people with Down's syndrome have been established in some areas because of the known risk of dementia. Without a baseline of typical functioning it is difficulty to monitor changes.

Screening and assessment

Referral routes and diagnostic processes are different in different localities. If your area has a dementia care pathway, this should be followed. The process of making a diagnosis may involve assessment by speech and language therapists, occupational therapists, physiotherapists, learning disability nurses, psychologists, psychiatrists, podiatrists and dieticians, with the person's GP being notified of the results. Diagnosis should include finding out information about recent life events, personality, level of previous functioning, a mental state examination (orientation to time, place, mood, sense of well-being), environmental assessment and physical health examination.

Assessment tools used for dementia diagnosis in the population generally are not appropriate for people with learning disabilities. For example, widely used tools such as the Mini-Mental State Examination (MMSE) or the Addenbrookes Cognitive Examination (3rd edition) assume a level of cognitive functioning that many people with a learning disability will not have even before dementia-related changes.

An example of a tool which has been used in screening is the NTG-EDSD (see further reading on p21). The tool is useful in early detection of dementia in people with a learning disability who are showing early signs. It may also be useful in monitoring change in the early stages of dementia, as well as detecting other health conditions. The tool is for use by staff and family carers and includes a self-report section for people with learning disabilities. It is not designed for use in diagnosis.

Other assessment measures for people with learning disabilities include:

- Adaptive Behaviour in Dementia Questionnaire (ABDQ). Available from: http://tidigatecken.se/ABDQ%20svensk%20version.pdf
- The Cambridge Examination for Mental Disorders of Older People with Down's Syndrome and Others with Intellectual Disabilities (CAMDEX-DS).
- Dementia Screening Questionnaire for Individuals with Intellectual Disabilities (DSQUIID). Available from: https://www.birmingham.ac.uk/documents/college-les/psych/ld/lddementiascreeningquestionnaire.pdf

It is important that the person with a learning disability remains involved in, and informed about, baseline assessments, screening and diagnosis. This can mean conversations which staff and volunteers find difficult or uncomfortable. Nevertheless, this is important and there are tools such as *Jenny's Diary* (see further reading) which can support this process.

Post-diagnostic support

Within dementia care generally, there is a growing emphasis on post-diagnostic support. This is equally important for people with a learning disability who are diagnosed with dementia. In 2016, an international summit on learning disability and dementia held in Scotland identified seven key areas for people with a learning disability who are diagnosed with dementia: post-diagnostic counselling; psychological and medical surveillance; regular reviews with adjustments to the care plan; early identification of behaviour and psychological changes; reviews of care practices with associated supports for advanced dementia and end of life; supports to carers and support staff; and evaluation of quality of life. The main contact for post-diagnostic support will vary from area to area: it may be learning disability services, or it may be older persons' or dementia care services. The former are usually best placed as the person is often already known to them.

Medication

Anecdotally, day-to-day use of anti-dementia medication such as Donepezil (Aricept) is reported to benefit some people with a learning disability. However, few studies have been conducted and the results are not consistent. Whilst being mindful of potential side effects, Aricept may still be offered to a person with a learning disability and dementia, unless they have medical conditions that rule this out (e.g. heart problems). Rivastigmine (Exelon) and Galantamine (Reminyl) work in a similar way to Donepezil, but one might suit a certain individual better than another, particularly in terms of side effects experienced.

Another anti-dementia drug that is available is Memantine (Ebixa/Maruxa/Nemdatine), usually given in the middle or late stage of dementia. A recent trial of Memantine given to people with dementia and Down's syndrome showed no benefit.

Whilst it is important to know about medication options, this self-study guide primarily focuses on non-drug supports for people with a learning disability and dementia.

Capacity

Dementia is a progressive condition, so the person will lose their ability to do various things over time. Skills needed to carry out certain activities and the ability to understand the world around them will diminish, however:

- These skills will not disappear all at once. People will retain insights and abilities to varying degrees. Therefore, we must allow and enable people to do things and make decisions about their life for as long as they have the ability and capacity to do this. For example, it may be that someone can no longer make decisions about their medical care, but they still can make decisions about where they live and the things they want to do.

- Capacity is not necessarily fixed by stage of dementia or severity of symptoms. Someone with a learning disability may lack capacity even before the onset of dementia, but this should not be assumed. Accessible ways of supporting people with a learning disability and dementia can enable, for example, participation in future planning.

The issue of capacity is covered by legislation. For example, in Scotland by the Adults with Incapacity Act (2000), in England and Wales by the Mental Capacity Act (2005) and in Northern Ireland by the Mental Capacity Act (2016).

Understanding the brain

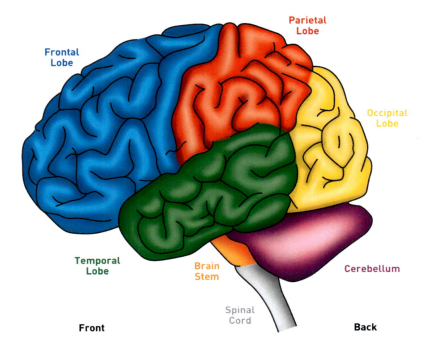

Figure 2: Regions of the human brain

Different parts of the brain control our feelings, memory and behaviour in different ways. Understanding the brain and the impact of dementia on it can help us understand and explain the changing behaviours that we see.

■ Temporal lobe

This lobe stores verbal memory on the left-hand side of the brain and the controls for seeing, smelling and tasting on the right-hand side. Both sides affect our ability to learn new things. If dementia damages this part of the brain, recent memory is lost.

■ Parietal lobe

The parietal lobes are on opposite sides of the brain. The right side helps us to find our way around and to understand where we are. When this side of the brain is damaged people will have problems with steps and stairs. Our language skill is stored on the left side, along with our arithmetic skills and our ability to understand our own bodies. If this area is damaged, people have difficulty managing money and dressing themselves.

- Frontal lobe

This lobe is where new learning takes place before going to the parietal lobes. It is where we plan, motivate ourselves and become organised. If this is damaged, the person with dementia may look as if they don't want to join in with activities, but if someone else prompts them to do so, they may be able to copy actions and may even need reminding to stop.

- Occipital lobe

This is the visual processing centre of the brain. Its functions include identifying colour and recognising objects. If this area of the brain is damaged, the person may experience hallucinations.

Understanding the 'reality' of a person with dementia

Understanding how the brain is affected is the first important step towards understanding how each person perceives the world – in other words, what their reality is. Short-term memory will typically fade, with the part of our brain that stores long-term memory generally remaining intact for longer. This means that the person does not always function in the present day, although this will vary between individuals and at different stages of dementia. Instead, they believe that they are functioning perfectly well in the reality that is their long-term memories. Because they believe they are in a different time and place, the person with dementia will have a different sense of what is 'real'.

- This can cause enormous stress and upset if the person has difficulty making sense of their environment, recognising the people around them, understanding spoken language (including dialect or accent if it is not in their long-term memory), knowing how old they are and what they should be doing.

- We need to understand the reality that each person is experiencing, to put ourselves as far as possible in their shoes. Without this understanding we cannot begin to know how best to provide support, what causes alarm or provides comfort and how best to communicate.

- Getting to know each person and their unique history is important in supporting people with a learning disability and dementia.

People with a learning disability and dementia: involvement and participation

Whilst it is important to consider the medical causes and symptoms of dementia, it is also important to consider social, emotional and physical environments. Environments, relationships, attitudes and service provision can be altered or developed so that day-to-day life is less stressful and more fulfilling. This means that relationship-based support (relationships between people with a learning disability and dementia, those who support or care for them, friends and community based supports) is significant.

It is important that people with a learning disability and dementia remain included and involved in decisions about their day-to-day care and support. They have a right to this now and in the future. There is much to be developed from the self-advocacy movement in learning disability and movements towards empowerment and inclusion of people with dementia, for example the DEEP network (see further reading on p21). Understanding from self-advocates in both movements demonstrates how people with a learning disability and dementia may be more actively involved in day-to-day life. However there is currently a lack of self-advocacy among people with learning disability and dementia.

Whilst there has been an increase in policy, plans and strategies specifically aimed at improving the lives of people with dementia, and separately of people with learning disabilities, current approaches to learning disability and dementia are mostly buried in the separate dementia or learning disability policy and plans. National dementia plans or strategies stop at identifying learning disability and dementia as an important issue for people with Down's syndrome. The specific challenges that people and their carers encounter are not addressed, nor are strategies for support typically suggested.

Social care or community-based staff may be familiar with supporting people who have a learning disability, but not dementia. Staff supporting people with dementia may not be familiar with what it means to have a learning disability. Staff and volunteers supporting both groups need support and training to understand issues around learning disability and dementia.

Key points

It is important to be able to recognise the early signs of dementia in people with a learning disability and to know where to go for support and diagnosis. We must not jump to conclusions and assume that a person has dementia when their condition may be caused by something else that is treatable. If a diagnosis of dementia is made, there are many ways in which the right support can lead to positive experiences. Chapters 2 to 9 explore this in more detail.

Links to the *Supporting Derek* film

- It is not stated if Theresa knows of Derek's diagnosis of dementia, and, if so, whether she has received training and support in this area. You might like to think about the issues relating to diagnosis and the recording of information in both scenarios.

- Derek's knowledge of his condition is not made clear, nor is Peter's. However, Peter's sympathetic tone and gentle insistence that he has previously told Derek what he must not do, suggests that he may have some awareness of what is causing Derek's changed behaviour or even that he has dementia. How can you support friends to accept the changed behaviour of their peers?

Activities

Activity 1

Think back to a time in your past and remember how you felt when you were younger. Now, imagine that you are in the present day, but your recollection is mainly of people and places from your past. Discuss how this may feel and which aspects of life today would not make sense to you.

Activity 2

Try to think about what the person you are supporting did when they were younger; this may be different from their recent activities. For example, they may have gone to church or taken part in religious activities that differ from their more recent practices. They may even have spoken a different language or grown up in a more institutional setting.

Activity 3

It is considered best practice, and a basic human right, to tell a person with dementia about their diagnosis. This is complicated if the person with a learning disability will not know what dementia means and these conversations need to be handled sensitively. Think about how you would want the conversations to be broached if you found yourself in that situation. Then think about how those conversations could be adapted to make the process accessible to people with a learning disability who you support. Do you always need to use the word dementia to tell someone that they are ill?

Further reading

BILD Easy Read Factsheets: http://www.bild.org.uk/resources/ageingwell/dementiafactsheets/

DEEP (The UK Network of Dementia Voices) http://dementiavoices.org.uk/

Dodd K, Watchman K, Janicki M, Coppus A, Gaertner C & Fortea J (2017) Consensus statement of the international summit on intellectual disability and dementia related to post diagnostic support. *Aging & Mental Health*. Epub ahead of print.

National Downs Syndrome Society (2018) *Alzheimer's Disease and Down Syndrome* [online]. Available at: https://www.ndss.org/wp-content/uploads/2018/04/NDSS_Guidebook_FINAL.pdf (accessed September 2018).

National Task Group on Intellectual Disabilities and Dementia Practices (NTG) NTG-EDSD Screening Instrument. Available at: http://aadmd.org/ntg/screening (accessed September 2018).

Public Health England (2018) *Dementia and People with Learning Disabilities* [online]. Available at: https://assets.publishing.service.gov.uk/government/uploads/system/uploads/attachment_data/file/716001/1_Dementia_and_people_with_learning_disabilities_making_reasonable_adjustments.pdf (accessed September 2018).

Watchman K. Learning Disability and Dementia International Summit Reports [online]. Available at: http://www.learningdisabilityanddementia.org/id-dementia-summit.html (accessed September 2018).

Watchman K (2015) *Jenny's Diary*. A booklet and set of postcards in a range of languages, available as a free download from: http://www.learningdisabilityanddementia.org/jennys-diary.html (accessed September 2018).

Watchman K (2017) *Intellectual Disabilities and Dementia. A guide for families*. London: Jessica Kingsley Publishers.

Watchman K & Strydon A (2018) Learning Disabilities and Dementia: Alzheimer's Society factsheet 430.

1A: Getting the right diagnosis

Treatable conditions causing changes that can be confused with dementia	Changes that may indicate the onset of dementia
■ Poor eyesight ■ Cornea inflammation ■ Hearing loss ■ Poor diet ■ Effects of medication ■ Recent bereavement ■ Significant change such as accommodation ■ Sleep apnoea ■ Early menopause in women with Down's syndrome ■ Compulsive disorders ■ Cardiac abnormalities ■ Osteoporosis ■ Cataracts ■ Urinary tract infection ■ Joint pain ■ Change in sleep pattern ■ Depression ■ Diabetes ■ Hypothyroidism ■ Coning of the cornea	■ Loss of road sense ■ Loss of interest in hobbies ■ Disorientation ■ New cognitive loss ■ Difficulty in finding the correct word ■ Difficulty with thresholds between rooms ■ Loss of daily living skills ■ Confused by steps or kerbs ■ Apathy ■ Attempting a task without realising it is not achievable ■ Not aware of having forgotten something ■ New short-term memory loss ■ Confusion ■ Loss of social skills ■ Deterioration in communication

Chapter 1: Understanding learning disability and dementia

Tool 1B: Diagnostic pathway

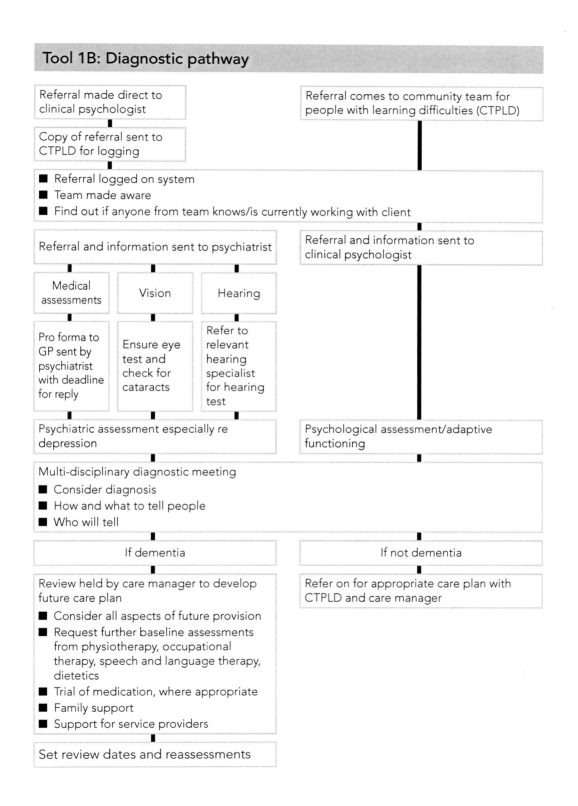

1C: Early signs

Most common changes associated with the early stages of dementia:
- loss of daily living skills
- short-term memory loss
- apathy and inactivity
- reduced sociability
- loss of interest in previously enjoyed hobbies
- lack of spontaneous communication
- disorientation and confusion
- poor comprehension
- appearing to wander for no reason
- difficulty with steps or kerbs.

Many of these signs may be present already, so it is important to note any evidence of deterioration that suggests the person may have dementia.

If someone shows three or more of these changes then a formal diagnosis should be sought.

Tool 1D: Understanding how the brain affects behaviour

Frontal lobe
- New learning takes place
- Planning and organising centre
- Judgement and impulse control
- Controls problem solving

Parietal lobe
Left side – analytical logical
- Controls patterning
- Use of language and numbers
- Management of money
- Recognition of body geography

Right side – 3D centre
- Location in space
- Identification of changes in levels and textures

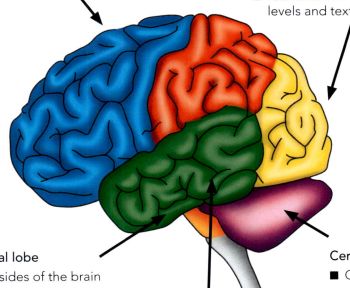

Temporal lobe
- Both sides of the brain
- Left side for verbal memory
- Right side for visual memory
- Smell and taste both sides
- Where we learn new things
- Recent memory recorder and filing system

Cerebellum
- Controls balance and co-ordination of voluntary movement such as walking and sitting

Hypothalamus
- Memory and learning
- First part affected in Alzheimer's

Limbic region
- Controls sleep, appetite and emotions

Chapter 2: Understanding behaviour

Chapter aim: to raise awareness that 'difficult' behaviour is not an inevitable consequence of dementia. It is usually caused by the environment or by interaction with other people.

When someone has dementia, we may at times find his or her behaviour unusual or difficult. There is always a reason for a person's altered behaviour and we need to find out what it is – sometimes we ourselves are the cause.

Reasons for changed behaviour

Potential reasons for changes in behaviour can include:

- an environment that is too confusing or noisy
- changes in communication
- mixing up day and night
- not recognising own reflection in mirrors
- not being able to eat without support, but being unable to express this appropriately
- forgetting where the bathroom is
- not having pain detected or treated
- not remembering where 'home' is, but needing to look for it
- not recognising current carers or friends, but looking for family or familiar people who may have died many years ago
- confusion or distress caused by remembering routines from when the person was younger, but not from recent months or years
- the effect of poor lighting and the design of the building

■ boredom resulting from lack of stimulating activity.

By linking the topics in this guide back to behaviour, we can start to identify the reasons for such changes. This core theme runs throughout the *Supporting People with Learning Disabilities and Dementia* training pack and this guide, because we know that behaviour can be changed by what we do, by medication, by buildings and by the environment.

Reflections in doors or windows can have the same effect as mirrors for a person with dementia.

Supporting changed behaviour

When we try to understand someone's behaviour it is important to consider that there may be more than one reason for that behaviour and that we may need to try different approaches:

- Make sure that medication is not used as a first response.
- Find out what has triggered the behaviour; what happened immediately before and what happened as a result.
- Try to understand what the person needs or wants to communicate to us.
- Look at it from the perspective of the person who has dementia; remembering that they are likely to be disorientated, frightened and confused.
- Alter our verbal communication methods.
- Alter our non-verbal communication methods.
- Use gentle touch.
- Use calming music if the person likes this.
- Provide an activity that the person enjoys, or another distraction.

Positive risk taking

People with learning disabilities have experienced numerous transition points throughout their life: starting and moving between schools, moving to adulthood and adult services, or changing accommodation. Getting older is a further transition and positive risk taking is no less important now than earlier in life. Positive risk taking is about the rights of an individual to make their own decisions and the role of their care team, family and friends in supporting them to do so safely. Even with dementia, risk can and should never be completely eliminated from someone's life, and ways should be discussed to positively manage and embrace it.

Key point

How we respond to a person's behaviour has been shown to be crucial in the care and support of a person with a learning disability and dementia.

Links to *Supporting Derek* film

- Derek is not alarmed by his reflection in the door or bathroom mirror, although he does not recognise himself. However, he is alarmed by the mirror in his bedroom and sees this as a 'man in there'. The mirror may reflect his image as he goes into the room or even something or someone outside his window, or elsewhere in his room. He believes that there is a stranger in his room.

- If someone's behaviour feels increasingly problematic for us we can often do things we would not ordinarily do. We may raise our voice, show our frustration in our body language or physically try to support people incorrectly (which Theresa did when helping Derek to his feet). It is important to acknowledge and control these frustrations and talk to a colleague or manager about them.

Activities

Activity 1

Discuss how you would feel if a stranger came into your home and started looking through your fridge and removing food.

Activity 2

Consider why Derek may be trying to leave the house to go to see his mum. Think about:
- What happened before. (Theresa helped him to get up with no appropriate cue that it was meal time. Seeing his coat in the hall reinforced his need to go outside.)
- What he did.
- What happened afterwards.
- What could have been done differently.

Activity 3

Think about the behaviour you find difficult in the people you support. Try to put yourself in the shoes of the person with a learning disability and dementia to look for an explanation. Consider the building you are in, how you approach the person, what time of day (or night) it is and who else is present.

Further reading

Alzheimer's Society (2014) Factsheet 525LP: Changes in Behaviour [online]. London: Alzheimer's Society. Available at: https://www.alzheimers.org.uk/download/downloads/id/3354/changes_in_behaviour.pdf (accessed September 2018).

British Psychological Society (2015) Dementia and People with Intellectual Disabilities: Guidance on the assessment, diagnosis, interventions and support of people with intellectual disabilities who develop dementia [online]. Leicester, UK: The British Psychological Society. Available at: https://www1.bps.org.uk/system/files/Public%20files/rep77_dementia_and_id.pdf (accessed September 2018).

Iacono T, Bigby C, Carling-Jenkins R & Torr J (2014) Taking each day as it comes: Staff experiences of supporting people with Down's syndrome and Alzheimer's disease in group homes. Journal of Intellectual Disability Research **58** (6) 521–533.

Jokinen N, Gomiero T, Hogan M, Larsen F, Berankova A, Santos F, Watchman K, Janicki M & Crowe J (2018) Challenges and perspectives in the caregiving of ageing people with intellectual disability affected by dementia: commentary from the International Summit on Intellectual Disability and Dementia. Journal of Gerontological Social Work **61** (4) 411–431.

Strydom A, Al-Janabi T, Houston M & Ridley J (2016) Best practice in caring for adults with dementia and learning disabilities. Nursing Standard **31** (6) 42–51.

Tool 2A: Understanding behaviour

- Is the environment too confusing or noisy?
- Are instructions clear and short?
- Are there visual prompts to remind the person if it is day time or night time?
- Is appropriate support given at meal times?
- Is it clear which door the toilet is behind?
- Could the person be in pain?
- Do you know where they think of as 'home'?
- Are you familiar with activities and routines from when the person was younger?
- Is the lighting and design appropriate for people with dementia?
- Who does the person look for when they are seeking familiar faces and what was the nature of their relationship?
- Is there enough choice over activities that are both stimulating and meaningful for the individual?

What happened before the behaviour?

Who else was there?

When did it happen?

Where did it happen?

What exact behaviour occurred?

What happened afterwards?

Tool 2B: Dealing effectively with changing behaviour

DO:
- stay calm
- use a calm voice
- touch the person gently, making sure they have seen you first
- turn off any music that has an agitating beat or high noise level
- use gentle, calming music
- give the person room to move or walk away
- offer reassurance
- try to divert attention.

DO NOT:
- confront the person
- shout or raise your voice
- say that a family member is dead, even if they are
- tease or make fun of someone
- invade their personal space
- move quickly, especially from behind
- corner the person.

Adrenalin stays in the body for up to 90 minutes. Even if a person has calmed down, this means that they may still be agitated or ready to display difficult behaviour again quickly. Try to keep the environment as calm as possible to prevent this from happening.

Chapter 3: Environment

Chapter aim: to identify ways in which the environment can be made enabling rather than disabling.

We are all influenced by our environment, but people with dementia can be more affected. The room size, heat level, arrangement and type of furniture, air quality, lighting and noise level will all have an impact on the way we work, live and relax. While we have a certain amount of control over these aspects of the environment, a person with dementia often does not. This is particularly problematic because the changes brought about by dementia mean that the environment can feel unpredictable, unfamiliar and distressing.

The increasing impairment associated with dementia means that people become more dependent on the structure of their environment to help them cope. They also become much more sensitive to their social, emotional and physical environment. It is not surprising, therefore, that much of the behaviour we see amongst people with dementia is caused by the ways carers act and by the environment.

Creating the right environment

There are five basic criteria for making sure that the environment in which people with dementia live, work and socialise does not have a negative effect on their well-being and, instead, maintains skills. It needs to:

- be calm
- be familiar
- be predictable
- make sense
- be appropriately stimulating.

Making suitable adaptations to the environment can reduce distress and behaviour that we, and the person, may find difficult. It may support someone to remain at home for longer, if that is their choice and in their best interests. However, there are advantages and disadvantages to changing the environment, and some changes may be too confusing if not implemented early enough.

Changes can be made in residential and family homes, and in community facilities, including GP surgeries and hospitals. Buildings are routinely designed or adapted for people with physical disabilities or those who are visually impaired, yet we do not routinely design or adapt the environment for people with dementia, despite knowing what can help. Of course, the needs of other residents must also be taken into account and this may be a careful balancing act, but even small changes can make a big difference.

Remember that what works for one person will not necessarily work for others. If one strategy does not work we need to keep trying, rather than thinking that nothing can be done. Knowing a persons' life story can help us to understand the differences needed by each individual.

The five criteria for creating a suitable environment are now explored in more detail with examples.

Calm

Because people with dementia are easily agitated, it is important that the environment has a calming effect.

- Noise levels should be reduced. People with dementia have difficulty in determining which noises to listen to and which to ignore.
- Noise levels that are acceptable for carers are often overwhelming for people with dementia. This includes the hoover, washing machine or people talking. Check that the radio or television is not turned on as 'background noise'.
- The environment should not contain too much activity. For example, often in day services there is a lot of movement and activity throughout the day. People with dementia may need to be in one place and have fewer activities (but not be excluded).
- A noisy environment is often the reason that a person with a learning disability stops attending college, the workplace, the resource day centre and places that they have enjoyed socially.

Chapter 3: Environment

The furniture shown is traditional. Attempts have been made to use signs, although this may not be the best way to meet Derek's needs. The pictures here are small and are not actual photographs of what is inside the cupboard.

Familiar

People with dementia can quickly feel abandoned and lost. As we have seen, loss of short-term memory means that their reality may be in their past. We do not often think about the furniture that a person with dementia has or the physical environment they are living in.

- Furniture may need to be traditional rather than modern. This means that it is familiar to the person, even though it may appear dated or old fashioned to us.

- Use traditional appliances as well, such as older clock faces (not digital), separate taps that are hot and cold (not mixer taps) and curtains rather than blinds.

- Ideally, the bathroom should have decor and toiletries that are recognisable to the person. If possible, you might like to offer a bath rather than a shower, as the shower might not be recognised.

- The ranges of flush options on modern toilets can be confusing. Often alarms in toilets are pulled by mistake.

- If the person has to move to another bedroom, try to mirror the decor, arrangements and scale so that it feels familiar.

Think about where and with whom the person with a learning disability and dementia grew up. This may give a clue to the type of furniture or surroundings that they recognise and feel comfortable with.

Predictable

People with dementia have increasing difficulty in recognising their environment. They cannot distinguish between the doors to their bedroom or the toilet, or remember what is behind the various doors in the kitchen. In most houses all doors are the same, which makes this problem more likely to occur. There are ways to create a more predictable environment so people can find their way.

- Good signage can help people find their way around. This applies to shops, GP surgeries, hospitals and community facilities, as well as to family or care homes.

- Photographs on cupboard and kitchen doors can be effective if they accurately show what is inside. This does rely on family members, staff or other residents always putting things back in the same place.

- Use colours to help recognition, especially colours such as red, orange and yellow, which are recognised for longer. Simple contrast can be created cheaply, for example by taping around light switches so they are easier to see.

- Use bed linen that is a plain but contrasting in colour to the floor and walls to help make the bed identifiable.

- Looking for bathrooms and toilets can cause distress (and apparent incontinence) if they are not clearly identified. Clear and consistent signage on the inside and outside of doors helps identify the way in and the way back out. Painting bathroom doors a contrasting colour or tone to the walls may be effective in highlighting the entrance.

- Use a contrasting coloured toilet seat to help make the toilet more recognisable from a distance. A dark or black toilet seat may be more recognisable to some, while a primary colour may be more visible to others.

- Help the person to locate the toilet at night by making it as visible as possible from the bed.

- Provide low lighting to guide someone to and back from toilet facilities at night.

- Ensure toilets can be easily viewed and accessed from the living and dining areas.

- Do not rearrange furniture, as this may cause confusion.
- Make the bedroom easily identifiable by colour and/or with a personal photograph or memory box outside.

The sign is clear, but the toilet door could be a different colour to contrast with the walls (also white) and sign. However, a red door would mean that the sign was less obvious. By having a contrasting painted door and a contrasting sign two approaches are being taken. Different people may respond better to one or the other.

Make sense

Because the person will have a changing sense of reality, and because dementia can cause difficulty seeing things in 3D, there are a number of aspects in the environment that do not always make sense. We need to understand these aspects, remembering that each person with dementia may view things differently.

- Remove or cover mirrors if they cause distress. The person may see their image and believe there is a stranger in the room. However, it may not always be necessary. Although the person may not recognise themselves, it may not upset them. Indeed, they may take comfort in seeing someone they perceive as a family member.

- Stepping across thresholds between rooms can cause problems. A difference in colour or flooring can appear as a step, especially if there is a shiny or different coloured strip between rooms.

- A contrast of floor colour between rooms or dark patterns on the carpet may appear as holes, which a person will go to lengths to avoid.

- Shiny floors, common in bathrooms or kitchens, can appear as water and should be avoided or replaced where possible.

- Shiny flooring can also be found in some buses and may lead to the person being reluctant to travel.

Going from a dark, complex patterned floor in one room to a light plain carpet in another room, and the shiny metal strip, can cause confusion.

Suitably stimulating

People with dementia are easily agitated by too much activity and are not able to begin activities for themselves, so there is a risk of them being under-stimulated and bored. The environment needs to provide the right level of stimulation.

- Outside views provide the opportunity to watch the world go by.
- Large low-level windows and well-positioned seating can provide stimulation. Position yourself where the person sits to check their view.

- The environment needs to allow for activities to take place in peaceful, undemanding settings.
- The room temperature should enable people to be active and awake, but also feel warm and secure.
- Light levels should be suitable for the activities.

Derek no longer recognises what to do with his mp3 player as this information is not in his long-term memory.

Independent and supported living

When we think about how the environment may be adapted, we should also consider the role that technology can play in supporting people with dementia.

People with a learning disability should always be supported to live in their own accommodation, if this is their choice. Independent living does not necessarily mean a person living on their own, although increasingly self-directed support is helping those who are able to do so. Self-directed support refers to people having access to appropriate support or technological interventions and the choice of whether to use them. Some people manage their support on their own, whereas others need help from family, friends or paid staff.

When someone with a learning disability develops dementia, their care needs will change. Without timely and appropriate interventions there is an increased likelihood of the person being moved, often in a crisis situation, into older people's services. In the case of people with Down's syndrome, they will then be significantly younger than other residents. Efforts should be made to avoid this. Where possible, changes to staffing and the environment are preferable to a move into a different care setting, which may not be appropriate for someone with a learning disability. A diagnosis of dementia should not automatically mean that a person has to move. Interventions to consider should include the use of telecare and telehealth.

Telecare

Telecare is the use of computerised or electronic devices that are connected electronically to a call centre, family carer or nearby staff member.

Telecare can take the form of community alarms, sensors that transmit information, environmental control systems or wireless capability with global positioning system (GPS). Examples include:

- a flood detector to alert if the bath overflows
- a door contact to alert a carer if a door is opened often or left open overnight
- an infra-red beam that transmits a signal if the person gets up at night
- a fall detector
- an enuresis monitor that alerts a carer if the person urinates in bed
- a seizure monitor
- a medication dispenser that reminds the person to take their medicine at the same time every day. The correct medication dose is automatically dispensed.

Telehealth

Telehealth also has the potential to be a support for a person with a learning disability and dementia. Such support can include medical checks carried out locally and transferred electronically to a doctor or nurse, who then advises by telephone if needed.

Telehealth may offer:

- remote care; for example, the collection of blood pressure, temperature or blood sugar levels in the person's home

- transmission of this information via a hand-held device, telephone or the internet
- clinical feedback on how to manage the condition
- reduced need for travel to appointments.

Implementing telecare and telehealth

- Some interventions may not be appropriate if the person is upset by loud noises or sudden voices, so individual needs must be considered. There are a number of other issues to consider before implementing the use of telecare or telehealth with people who have a learning disability and dementia.
- As part of the care planning, an assessment should be carried out with the person with a learning disability and then separately with their carer if they live with one.
- Some forms of telecare or technology require internet access, which may not be available to the individual. Alternative low-tech interventions should be considered in such situations.
- National guidance on capacity and consent should be followed.
- The degree of risk should be considered in relation to the increased mobility, independence and choice that telecare may offer.
- The person may choose not to use any form of telecare even after any possible risks associated with not doing so have been explained.
- Informed consent requires good communication between the carer and person with a learning disability. Be aware of any non-verbal cues that may suggest that the person is upset.
- Telecare or telehealth should not be a substitute for non-technological interventions, particularly contact with other people, or staff, especially at night.
- Telecare equipment should be checked regularly, and batteries replaced if needed. It should be clear who is responsible for this and other maintenance.
- If a decision is made on behalf of someone who lacks the capacity to make choices for themselves this must be time-limited, reviewed regularly and limited to the specific service or use of equipment.
- Regardless of whether telecare is to be introduced, consideration should be given to ensure that people with a learning disability are not digitally excluded. For example, social care providers should endeavor to ensure that

residents in the facility have WiFi access and know how to use this to improve their quality of life

Key points

Attention should be paid to the physical environment where an individual with a learning disability lives, works or socialises. Whilst respecting individual preferences, the environment should be calm, familiar, predictable, make sense and be appropriately stimulating.

Links to the *Supporting Derek* film

- There is no cue or sign from the lounge to show Derek which door to go through to find, or return from, the toilet. This can result in people with dementia urinating in inappropriate places. This is not an inevitable consequence of dementia; it is due to a reduced capacity to find the way, lack of cues from staff or the environment and the effect of long-term memory retention.

- Derek's bedroom door is the same colour as the other bedroom and bathroom doors. This is also the same colour as the walls in this part of the house, so he is unable to identify his own room. A memory box or familiar photographs could be placed on the outside of his door so that he knows which room is his.

- The room is very noisy when we first meet Derek. The television is playing loudly and Theresa is walking and talking on a mobile phone. The level of noise, which may appear normal in most houses, resource centres or community buildings, will be overwhelming to the senses of a person with dementia, making communication almost impossible.

- Technology has impacted on Derek and Peter in different ways. For example, Peter is able to listen to the television through wireless headphones without Derek being affected by the noise.

- Derek used his mp3 player until fairly recently. Now he holds it, but has no recollection of what to do with it. This is because his short-term memory has been affected too severely and in his long-term memory such technology was not available. The mp3 player has become unrecognisable to him. This does not mean that he cannot still enjoy music, such as an individualised playlist that staff can play for Derek which may prove calming if he becomes agitated.

Activities

Activity 1

Consider the most recent opportunity you had to visit a place for the first time. What cues did you look for to find your way around? What would you do in a hotel if there were no numbers on the doors? How would you find your bedroom?

Activity 2

Discuss the signage in your workplace or signs that you have seen elsewhere. Think about the style, and position, how appropriate they are and what may be changed as the needs of people with a learning disability and dementia change.

Activity 3

Discuss how the home of a person you know could be adapted to support a person who has a learning disability and dementia.

Further reading

Forbat L and Wilkinson H (2008) Where should people with dementia live? Using the views of service users to inform models of care. *British Journal of Learning Disabilities* **36** (1) 6–12.

Watchman K (2006) *Living with Dementia: Adapting the home of a person who has Down's syndrome and dementia – a guide for carers* [online]. Edinburgh: Down's Syndrome Scotland. Available at: http://www.learningdisabilityanddementia.org/uploads/1/1/5/8/11581920/living-with-dementia.pdf (accessed September 2018).

Wilkinson H, Kerr D & Rae C (2004) *Home for Good?* [online]. York: The Joseph Rowntree Foundation. Available at: https://www.jrf.org.uk/report/support-people-learning-difficulties-residential-settings-who-develop-dementia (accessed September 2018).

National Task Group on Intellectual Disabilities and Dementia Practice (2012). *'My Thinker's Not Working': A national strategy for enabling adults with intellectual disabilities affected by dementia to remain in their community and receive quality support* [online]. Available at: https://aadmd.org/sites/default/files/NTG_Thinker_Report.pdf (accessed September 2018).

Chapter 4: Responding to pain

Chapter aim: to raise awareness that a person with a learning disability and dementia is likely to have high levels of undiagnosed and untreated pain.

As people get older they are more likely to experience pain, particularly chronic pain. People with dementia may find it hard to tell others when they are in pain, where the pain is and how bad it is. Therefore, it is important that we are aware of this and are able to provide appropriate responses. Take the time to understand how individuals with a learning disability and dementia experience pain, how they express it and how we can anticipate it. It is a myth that people with a learning disability, including people with Down's syndrome, do not feel pain, or have a high pain threshold. It is how this pain is communicated that may differ.

Detecting pain

People with dementia may appear to tolerate or not recognise pain. This does not mean that they are not suffering; it may just mean that their pain has to worsen before anyone realises. Pain detection is made difficult by:

- loss of vocabulary and difficulty finding the right words to express pain
- a lack of understanding about how the body works.

People with dementia may lose the cognitive skills to remember left from right and confuse parts of the body, even if they know the correct general area.

For example, the mouth may be confused with the eyes or the abdomen may be confused with the chest. As a result, the person may find it difficult to identify the part of their body that hurts. So, if they have a toothache they might not be able to find the word to express this and may also be unable to indicate where the pain is. Or they may point out that someone else is in pain, when in fact it is them.

Undiagnosed pain leads to behaviour that we may not understand. It is very easy for us to blame the dementia or the person for their behaviour, rather than considering that this may be caused by their pain.

Chapter 4: Responding to pain

When someone is in pain we may see all or some of the following:

- fidgeting
- crying
- rocking
- shouting
- pacing
- becoming withdrawn
- heavy breathing
- knees pulled up
- confusion
- aggression
- screaming
- difficulty eating
- night-time waking
- hitting
- swearing
- groaning.

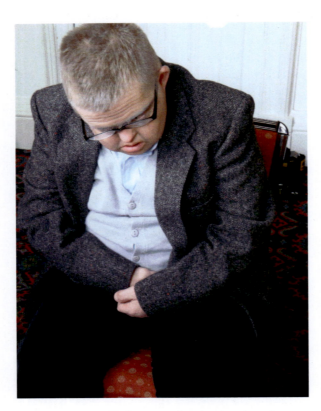

Derek's non-verbal signs of pain are clear here even if it is not his stomach that is hurting him. It is not always so obvious when a person with dementia is in pain.

What can we do?

There are things that can be done to identify, diagnose and treat pain in a person with a learning disability and dementia.

- To help decide if the person is in pain, and what may be causing it, we can use tools developed for this purpose, such as DisDAT (see further reading on p48).
- We should get into the habit of asking whether this could be pain, rather than making assumptions about someone's behaviour.
- It is important to know an individual's pain thresholds.
- Regularly updating the person's care plan will help to incorporate all aspects of care and reinforce the importance of exercise, physical activity and pain relief for joints and muscles.
- Do not wait to be told by the person that pain medication is needed, as this is unlikely to happen. Instead, anticipate this and give pain relief and see if this brings about a change. This is standard practice in a palliative care approach.
- Talk to their GP about giving pain relief regularly and routinely if pain is suspected.
- Monitor how much the person is eating and drinking to keep track of their nutrition and hydration.
- Consider the furniture – the person may be uncomfortable if their legs do not reach the floor or they are not well supported in a chair.
- Check the person's teeth and gums for disease or infection and establish whether the person's false teeth fit well.
- People with some forms of learning disability, such as Down's syndrome, have a narrow ear canal and are more likely to have impacted ears, so these need regular checking.

Key point

Knowing that people with a learning disability and dementia will experience high levels of unrecognised and untreated pain should make us much more pro-active in the support that we provide.

Link to *Supporting Derek* film

Derek's pain is not noticed by Theresa, who is preoccupied with the meal preparation.

Activities

Activity 1

Consider the different types of pain you feel, the words that you use to describe it, how it makes you feel and what treatment you seek.

Activity 2

Consider non-verbal ways that we may convey pain. Do we look for the same signs in people with a learning disability and dementia? Encourage empathy with the person with dementia who is unable to put this into words.

Activity 3

Think of a person you support who has a learning disability and dementia. What verbal and non-verbal signs of pain do they show and what is the reaction of staff to this?

Further reading

Abbey J, De Bellis A, Pillar N, Esterman A, Giles, L, Parker D and Lowcay D (2002) Abbey Pain Scale. Adelaide: JH and JD Gunn Medical Research Foundation. Available at: http://prc.coh.org/PainNOA/Abbey_Tool.pdf (accessed September 2018).

Joseph Rowntree Foundation Findings (2006) *Pain Management for Older People with Learning Difficulties and Dementia*. Available at: https://www.jrf.org.uk/report/pain-management-older-people-learning-difficulties-and-dementia (accessed September 2018).

Massachusetts General Hospital. *Pain Assessment in Advanced Dementia (PAINAD) Tool Guidelines*. Massachusetts: Massachusetts General Hospital. Available at: http://geriatrictoolkit.missouri.edu/cog/painad.pdf (accessed September 2018).

Northumberland Tyne and Wear NHS Trust and St. Oswald's Hospice (2008) Disability Distress Assessment Tool. DisDAT. Available at: http://prc.coh.org/PainNOA/Dis%20DAT_Tool.pdf (accessed September 2018).

Posters and factsheets available free to download from the above Joseph Rowntree Foundation website. Available at: https://www.jrf.org.uk/report/do-you-recognise-pain-someone-learning-difficulty-and-dementia (accessed September 2018).

Chapter 4: Responding to pain

Tool 4: Pain detection

Pain is often ignored or mistaken for behavioural problems

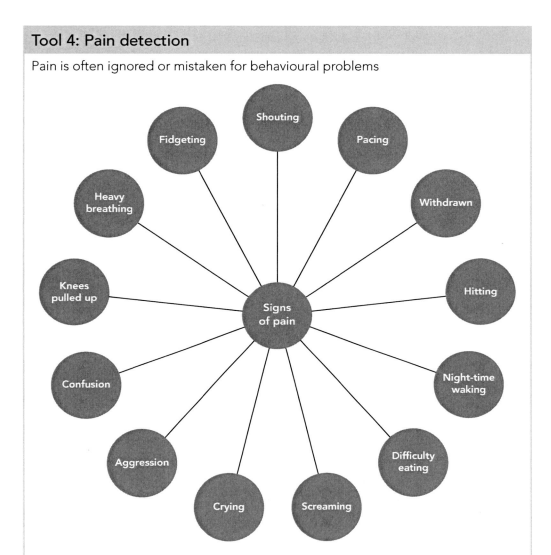

Common causes of chronic or acute pain that often untreated and unrecognised:
- joint pain
- urinary tract infection
- painful gums or teeth
- constipation
- impacted ear wax
- eye infection
- cellulitis
- arthritis

Chapter 5: Effective communication

Chapter aim: to highlight the changes in communication that may occur, and the associated change needed in our approach.

A person's ability to communicate verbally will change as dementia progresses. Such changes do not mean that the person is not able to communicate at all. A two-way conversation (verbal or non-verbal) may not still be possible, but meaningful communication is still both possible and essential. As dementia progresses, new communication methods must be sought and maintained. It is important that we do not give up trying to communicate. This is especially important if a change in accommodation has taken place, as new carers must understand the preferred communication method and ensure all other staff are aware.

People with dementia still want to communicate and they increasingly do so through their behaviour. We should focus on supporting the person to maintain their interests for as long as possible and maximise our use of non-verbal communication. Having an understanding and knowledge of the person before their dementia will help, as will spending time with them to 'tune into' their current communication. It will be helpful to keep the staff group supporting the person as small as possible, so there is greater familiarity and consistency in interactions.

It is important that all of the aids to good practice previously used to support someone with a learning disability are not lost or unused if they develop dementia. Essential Lifestyle Plans (ELPs), Hospital Passport, Making Action Plans (MAPs), Planning Alternative Tomorrows with Hope (PATHS), Communication Passport and Circles of Support should all still be used as part of a person-centred approach to future planning.

Changes in communication

The following verbal changes may be noted at different stages in people with dementia:

- difficulty in finding the correct word
- a different speech pattern

- repeating words or phrases
- a change in how words are pronounced
- consistently talking a lot more or less than usual
- an increase in shouting
- difficulty following a conversation.

Non-verbal changes in communication may also be noted at different stages:

- confusion and a lack of understanding shown in facial expression
- lack of motivation to follow direction
- appearing flustered or upset
- increased crying
- wringing of hands
- picking at skin
- reduced activity
- modelling behaviour – this means following or copying another resident or staff member.

Support with communication

It is important to be aware of, and monitor, any sensory changes that the person is experiencing, as this can impact on communication. For example, hearing loss can affect many people with Down's syndrome. This may be as a result of increased incidence of chronic ear disease or differences in the structure of the ear. Not responding to requests or conversation may be misinterpreted as an early sign of dementia, when in reality a hearing check can resolve this issue.

We must consider responses and think about where and when communication is taking place. There are ways in which we can support a person with dementia to communicate, both verbally and non-verbally:

- Turn towards the person when speaking and maintain eye contact.
- Smile when speaking.
- Use a friendly tone of voice (sometimes the person with dementia will hear only the tone rather than what is actually said).

- Use short sentences.
- Do not speak to anyone else at the same time.
- Speak in the same language that the person uses and understands (remember that someone with dementia may revert to the language that they spoke as a child as this will be in their long-term memory).
- Do not give more than one message or request in one sentence.
- Do not touch the person from behind without being seen, as this may cause alarm.
- Do not be embarrassed by silences (silences do not necessarily mean that the person has not understood). Often a person with dementia will make an appropriate response to a conversation many minutes later, after a prolonged period of silence.
- Talk to the person at the same eye level or lower, rather than looking down on them, as this may seem threatening.
- Make sure that the room or environment is quiet.

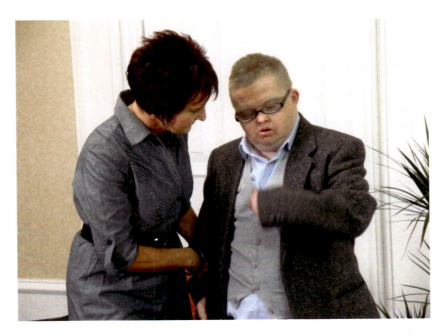

Derek pushes Theresa away as she tries to stop him from going 'home'.

Key point

Even though people with a learning disability are likely to have had an existing communication disability, we still need to develop new strategies and ways of understanding them if they have dementia.

Links to *Supporting Derek* film

- Theresa talks quickly and says a lot as she helps Derek in the hall. He will not be able to pick out what is important from her speech and will become increasingly confused. It is often assumed that this confusion, or even aggression, is caused by dementia. Staff do not realise that they can often do something about it by changing their approach.

- Theresa has a strong accent and uses local dialect, which may be difficult for the person with dementia to interpret. In this situation, Derek may need to use his other senses to try to understand what is required of him and focus more on Theresa's body language and facial expressions.

Further reading

Alzheimer's Society (2015) *Communicating and Language* [online]. Available at: https://www.alzheimers.org.uk/about-dementia/symptoms-and-diagnosis/symptoms/communicating-and-language (accessed September 2018).

Bradshaw J (2013) *Communication and Challenging Behaviour – information sheet* [online]. Available at: http://www.challengingbehaviour.org.uk/learning-disability-files/04---Communication-Information-sheet-web.pdf (accessed September 2018).

Royal College of Speech and Language Therapists (2013) *Five Good Communication Standards* [online]. Available at: https://www.rcslt.org/news/docs/good_comm_standards (accessed September 2018).

Talking Mats® have developed a range of resources to support staff and families working with people with communication disability: www.talkingmats.com.

The Dementia Engagement and Empowerment Project (DEEP) (2014) *Dementia Words Matter: Guidelines on language about dementia* [online]. Available at: http://dementiavoices.org.uk/wp-content/uploads/2015/03/DEEP-Guide-Language.pdf (accessed September 2018).

Tool 5: Verbal and non-verbal cues

Verbal and non-verbal changes in communication that may occur	Suggestions for verbal and non-verbal communication
■ Difficulty in finding the right word ■ Unusual speech pattern ■ Repeating words ■ Changing pronunciation of words ■ Increase in shouting ■ May forget recently learned Makaton signs ■ Becoming flustered ■ Picking at skin ■ Becoming more upset ■ Losing track of a conversation ■ Constantly talking more or less ■ Wringing of hands	■ Make eye contact ■ Smile while speaking ■ Use a friendly tone of voice ■ Use short sentences ■ Speak in the same language as the person with dementia ■ Do not be afraid of silence, this can be thinking time ■ Do not give too many messages at the same time ■ Do not use defensive or aggressive body language ■ Talk to someone at their eye level ■ Make sure the room is quiet ■ Do not speak to anyone else at the same time ■ Do not touch the person from behind

People with dementia still want and need to communicate.

To support this we must pick up on and return their cues.

Remember, a large part of our communication is non-verbal.

Chapter 6: Meaningful activities

Chapter aim: to increase knowledge about the range of activities that may prove meaningful to a person with dementia.

Activity will remain important to people with dementia but skills and ability to engage with them will change. In this section we have included examples of outdoor activities, music and the role of life-story work, but any activity will only be meaningful if it is important to the individual. People with dementia will become noticeably less able to start activities for themselves, although they may still want to do so. As a result, they will become increasingly bored or frustrated, which can lead to behaviour that we find difficult. We can support people to take part in activities they find easier, that are appropriate to their abilities and which can help to maintain skills or social relationships. This means that the activities must be:

- failure free, so that the person can feel they are accomplishing something without the fear or embarrassment of making mistakes
- enjoyable
- uncomplicated
- tailored to individuals.

Pressure should not be placed on someone to move from room to room, for example in a day or resource centre, to take part in different activities. This, along with the confusion and the noise of a number of people moving around at the same time, can prove stressful for people with dementia.

Where possible, the activity should go to the person, so that they can continue it if they are enjoying it, rather than feeling pressure to change activities because others do. We should not be prescriptive about the kind of activities that people are invited to join in with, as preferences will vary. Choices may include:

- Group or individual reminiscence activities.
- Life story work.

- Craft or art.
- One-to-one and group discussions and conversations.
- Domestic tasks, which often prove to be more enjoyable than more formal and structured activities, as they remind people of what they did when they were younger, and reinforce that they still have skills to contribute.
- Music playlists. Using an mp3 player can be more accessible, does not require an online account and allows for individualised preferences, although not everyone may be comfortable using headphones.

While following familiar rules can help some, this may eventually become problematic. As dementia progresses, activities should be repetitive and require minimal instruction. Caution is urged, as an effective and successful intervention for one person, may be less positive, or even distressing for another. For example, it should not be assumed that everyone will benefit from reminiscence activities, especially if negative memories are recollected.

Outdoor activities

For an activity to be meaningful there may be a link to something that the person enjoyed doing in their past. Meaningful activity can include being able to look at the garden, which should ideally contain plants, birds, ornaments or animals – even a washing line – as well as safe areas for walking and sitting. Making use of outdoor areas can aid well-being and health. Some people may enjoy community outdoor activities, walking, sports or visiting places of interest. Outdoor activities will have the additional benefit of boosting vitamin D levels.

An outside space does not have to be large, but should have level access to and from the building and around the garden itself. If there are steep pathways, a handrail should be in place. There are other issues to consider when we think about outdoor areas:

- Tables and seating areas allow games or reminiscence activities to take place outdoors as well as indoors.
- Plants should not be poisonous and should offer different scents, sounds and colours at different times of year.
- Consider the use of garden tools or equipment, such as a washing line and pole for hanging clothes.

- If space allows, a safe, enclosed area for walking, with seating at regular intervals, will let the person walk safely.
- Just sitting watching birds, trees, weather or activity in the street can be a meaningful activity for some people.
- If someone is using a wheelchair to go outdoors, it is important to ensure that they are comfortable in it.

When a person has dementia, the ability to enjoy outdoor space is essential, whether this is a garden, window box, balcony or patio area. Derek may have increasing difficulty with the garden steps, despite the handrail.

Music

An appropriate style of music can have a positive impact on the well-being of people with a learning disability and dementia.

- People can get enormous pleasure from familiar and personalised songs or playlists, whether on an mp3 player, iPod, CD or online media such as YouTube, iTunes or Spotify.
- Music does not place the same cognitive demands on a person as conversation, so people with dementia are able to retain knowledge of music long after other skills, including speech, have disappeared.
- People who are unable to find the words to complete a sentence can often sing an entire song word perfectly.
- For people with dementia who were sung to when they were younger, music can recreate feelings of safety, security and affection.
- Music should not be left on as background noise all day, as this can become irritating for others as well as the person with dementia. Make sure it is the type of music that the person wants to listen to rather than the choice of the staff member.
- We should not feel embarrassed about singing to, or with, a person who has dementia.

Life-story work

Life-story work helps to develop the story of someone's background and is essential for us to understand what they were like when they were younger. By knowing their past we start to understand their present. This can help to understand what activities may be meaningful to the individual. As short-term memory fades, the person's long-term memory becomes increasingly important; it is important to know about where they grew up, and who with. The information helps us to understand the person and creates a life story that can be used as a key form of communication. Different approaches can be taken.

- Flexibility is important; life-story work can be in the form of a book or album, but it does not have to be. A memory box containing important items from the past, such as toys, pictures, ornaments, hats, handbags, jewelry and photographs, can all help us understand a person's past. It should be remembered that life-story work, in any format, remains the property of the individual.

- There are a range of applications (apps) for mobile devices that can support digital life-story work. This is dependent on the person with a learning disability having internet access wherever they call home.

- A brief booklet or personal passport containing key information can move with the person and is especially useful during a short-term hospital stay or short break (respite care), where, with permission, it can be read quickly and easily by carers to assist communication.

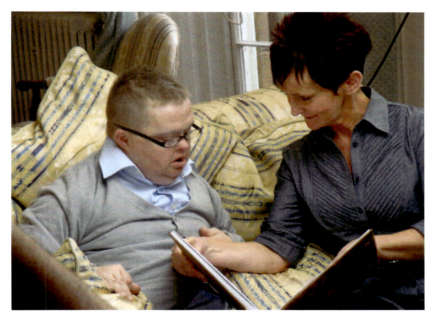

Looking at old family photographs on a one-to-one basis becomes a meaningful activity for Derek and one he can join in with.

Chapter 6: Meaningful activities

If a photo album is used for reminiscence or life story work this must include details of the person, place and activity so that the photographs can be used for as long as possible, even as dementia progresses.

Benefits of life-story work

- Carers can better understand the personality and history of a person with dementia.

- Helps carers have higher expectations of the person and interact more if they move to a new setting.

- Encourages positive interaction by identifying experiences that carers can talk about.

- Promotes communication; not speaking about memories does not mean that there are not any, or that the person will not enjoy hearing someone else describe past events in their life.

Night care staff and agency or bank staff need to have access to the same information, if the person is happy for it to be shared. All staff need to know where to access this information and its regular use should be encouraged.

Cautions for life-story work

- Life-story work can also remind someone of negative experiences. It is important for carers to know about these, as it can help them understand behaviour which may otherwise be seen as problematic. Distressing memories should not be pursued. Sounds, smells or activities that are known to bring back negative memories should be avoided. It should not be assumed that what works for one person with a learning disability and dementia will work for another.

- Life-story work should start as soon as possible, ideally before dementia is diagnosed. Try to include information from as many family members or former carers as possible.

- People with a learning disability may no longer have living parents and they may have little contact with siblings. Try other sources to find out background information, such as peers, a partner and former staff or carers.

- Life-story work should be viewed as an ongoing process not a one-off task, and it should be revisited and updated as often as the person wishes.

Key point

Despite the changes and cognitive losses that accompany dementia, there are many failure-free activities and interventions that can help someone maintain their quality of life for longer.

Links to *Supporting Derek* film

- Derek's life-story book is an album that contains photographs and text. Scanning photographs and storing them in a computer may help preserve photographs in the longer term. Memory books or albums can be created online and the use of digital photography can support ongoing life-story work.

- Derek has an MP3 player, which suggests that he enjoys listening to music. Rather than putting the television on during meal times, calming music may be beneficial and help him enjoy his meals.

- Derek grew up in his family home, so long-term recollections will be based on this and what he did when he was younger. Not all people with learning disabilities who grew up in the 1950s or 1960s, as Derek did, were encouraged to live independently or have a job. His choice of music, television, furniture and decor could have been influenced by his parents (or by staff, depending on where he lived) and reflect their generation rather than, or in addition to, Derek's.

Activities

Activity 1

Think about your early memories and what you would like others to know about you in the future.

Activity 2

How can you find out the activities that each individual you support may have enjoyed when they were younger? How can this be adapted to a meaningful activity for that person now that they have dementia? This may involve domestic tasks, such as light housework or gardening, setting a table or folding laundry.

Activity 3

What approach does your organisation take to life-story work? Is there a procedure for gathering background information before a person moves in or begins to use the service? If not, plan how this may look and how carers and people with a learning disability and dementia may be involved. If this exists already, plan how it may be improved and made easier to update.

Further reading

Fray M (2000) *Caring for Kathleen: A sister's story about Down's syndrome and dementia*. London: British Institute of Learning Disabilities.

Kiddle H, Drew N, Crabbe P & Wigmore J (2016) A pilot memory cafe for people with learning disabilities and memory difficulties. *British Journal of Learning Disabilities* **44** (3) 175–181.

MacIntyre (2014) *Hot Tips for Activities…a Starting Point* [online]. Available at: https://www.macintyrecharity.org/download/file/343/ (accessed September 2018).

Playlist for Life: https://www.playlistforlife.org.uk/

Shivers C, McCarron M, Mccallion P & Dinsmore J (2014) Acceptability of a multimedia life stories platform in a residential home for individuals with dementia and intellectual disability [online]. *Journal of Applied Research in Intellectual Disabilities* **27** (4) 397–398. Available at: http://iassidd2014.univie.ac.at/uploads/media/Shivers-Acceptability_of_a_multimedia_life_stories_plattform_in_a_residential_home.pdf (accessed September 2018).

Ward A & Parkes J (2017) An evaluation of a Singing for the Brain pilot with people with a learning disability and memory problems or a dementia. *Dementia* **16** (3) 360–374.

Tool 6A: Life story work: helping you learn the 'reality' of the person you support

Do you know:
- the person's background – where they grew up and who with?
- what they liked to do when they were younger?
- their favourite food and drink?
- food and drink they do not like?
- if they like to sing and, if so, what songs?
- what activities or responsibilities they enjoyed when younger?
- the sounds or smells that may cause upset or may provoke happy memories?
- if there is contact with family?
- what type of dementia the person has?
- what the person says if they are upset or in pain?
- what non-verbal clues the person gives if they are upset or in pain?
- how the person communicated before they had dementia?
- if life-story work has been started and, if so, where it is kept?
- who will discuss end-of-life care and in what way?
- what the person has been told about the changes they are experiencing and the words that were used to explain this?

Knowing all of this will help you know the reality of the person you are supporting and to plan with them for their future.

Tool 6B: Suggestions for life-story work

Areas to talk about and record:
- good times
- achievements
- important people, now and in the past
- hobbies, now and in the past
- places stayed in
- holidays
- religious or cultural interests
- relationships
- favourite songs
- likes and dislikes
- hopes and wishes
- favourite sayings.

Use a life story or memory box as well as a life-story book. Include a variety of things, such as:
- pictures
- labelled photographs
- music, CDs, DVDs
- programmes or tickets
- ornaments
- soft toys
- dolls
- fabrics
- things with a familiar scent.

Chapter 7: When a friend has dementia

Chapter aim: to understand the importance of maintaining relationships for a person with a learning disability and dementia and the supportive role that family and friends can play.

Friendships

Friends can play a pivotal role in providing support after a major health diagnosis such as dementia, through to the end of life. However, friends will also require support themselves. The degree and type of support will vary depending on the relationship to the person with dementia. Increasingly people with a learning disability are married or in long-term relationships. In such circumstances, support should be provided independently of the support provided for the partner with a diagnosis of dementia.

Friendships and social relationships are important to us all. For a person with a learning disability and dementia, relationships may include:

- Long-term friends, whose expertise may come from years of knowing and supporting the person.
- Peers: people with a learning disability (and possibly dementia too), in a group home.
- Peers in other contexts, such as self-advocacy groups.
- Colleagues and co-workers in paid or voluntary work settings.
- Formal carers, staff and volunteers, who are often the most constant person in the lives of some people with learning disabilities.

Staff are often the first to report changes happening, although friends may have noticed sooner. It is important that staff are aware of how much a friend or partner knows about dementia and about what is happening to the person. They may be able to share information about the person when they were younger (or may know who to ask) to help with life-story work and background information. Friends are likely to be very anxious about the future, for themselves as well as for the person.

Dementia can be difficult to talk about, but it is important that everyone remains open to communicating about it. It is important for staff and volunteers to be equipped in supporting relationships between peers. This support needs to be ongoing, not a one-off discussion or group information session. A person with a learning disability may be familiar with the term 'dementia' or 'Alzheimer's' and its implications; some may have parents or grandparents with dementia. It is important for staff to consistently use whichever term the person is already familiar with.

Consent to share information about a diagnosis with their friends can be a barrier – but staff can discuss dementia in general, if not specific, terms. Where possible staff and volunteers should support someone with a learning disability to visit a friend or family member with dementia who may have moved to new accommodation, whether temporary or permanent. This includes a hospital or a hospice.

It is important to continue to celebrate birthdays and religious festivals for the person who has dementia. The celebrations may need to be quieter and less active than previous years, but should still involve friends.

Support provided by staff for family and friends can take many different forms:

- Sharing information in a way that is clear and non-medical. This includes using accessible information about dementia to build on any knowledge that they may already have. An example is *Jenny's Diary: A resource to support conversations about dementia with people who have learning disabilities* (see further reading).
- Explaining that their relationship will change, and that this is not anyone's fault.
- Reinforcing the continued importance of their relationship.
- Explaining why the person with dementia may not always recognise them.
- Assisting them to acknowledge and understand the changing behaviour in their friend or family member.
- Helping to understand why the person's behaviour is changing.
- Explaining why staff need to spend more time with the person who has dementia.
- Addressing the concerns of peers who may worry that they, or other friends and family, will also develop dementia.

- Explaining why their friend's behavior is changing and why they are becoming more introverted or detached; less inhibited; or less willing to go out.

The friendship between Derek and Peter can be supported for as long as possible if both are aware of the changes being experienced by Derek.

Theresa talked to Peter to help him understand what was happening to Derek.

Often the person with a diagnosis of dementia is aware that something is wrong, although they may not understand what it is. It is important to acknowledge their changes in health using terms that will be understood, even if the word 'dementia' is not understood. This should then be followed with an explanation of the help and support that will be put in place.

Towards and during the end of life

Friends need support right up to, and after, the death of the person with dementia. This may include:

- Enabling hospital or hospice visits if the person would like to do this, so that their friend or family member who has dementia does not just disappear.
- Giving information about death and funerals based on the culture of the person.
- Offering choice over whether to attend or contribute to a funeral.
- Encouraging and displaying photographs or mementos of the person who has died.

- Supporting memorial activities, perhaps a service, or talking about the person who has died on future birthdays and festivals.
- Bereavement counselling, if appropriate.

Key point

Relationships remain extremely important to people with a learning disability, even as dementia progresses. Talking about the diagnosis with friends, in the most appropriate way for individuals, and using the same terms used to talk to the person with the diagnosis, should become part of ongoing support.

Links to *Supporting Derek* film

Peter and Derek have lived together for many years, yet Peter may not have been given an explanation for the changes Derek is experiencing. Providing support for Derek is taking up an increasing amount of Theresa's time, so Peter is often left on his own, as we see during the meal time. If Peter does not understand the situation there is potential for him to become resentful of Derek.

It is not clear in the film whether Derek's mother is still alive and if his desire to see his mum is realistic.

Activities

Activity 1

Think about how much information or explanation you would want to know about your health as you age. Would you want the same information about a family member or friend?

Activity 2

Discuss how much the people with a learning disability you support may already know about dementia, possibly as a result of previous experience among family or friends. If this is not known, how will you find out?

Activity 3

Consider small group discussions or one-on-one time that may be needed for people with a learning disability, to explain the changing health needs of their friends based on the information already given to the person with dementia.

Further reading

Foundation for People with Learning Disability (2015) *Talking Together: Facilitating peer support activities to help people with learning disabilities understand about growing older and living with dementia*. Available at: https://www.mentalhealth.org.uk/learning-disabilities/publications/talking-together (accessed September 2018).

Lindmeier B (2014) Support to co-residents of people with dementia and intellectual disability in group homes. *Journal of Applied Research in Intellectual Disabilities* **27** (4) 321.

Towers C & Wilkinson H (2014) Planning ahead: Supporting families to shape the future after a diagnosis of dementia. In: K Watchman (ed) *Intellectual Disability and Dementia* (p.161-182). London: Jessica Kingsley Publishers.

Waight M & Oldreive W (2013) Helping service users to understand dementia. *Learning Disability Practice* **16** (7) 16–20.

Watchman K, Tuffrey-Wijne I & Quinn S (2015) *Jenny's Diary: Supporting conversations about dementia with people who have a learning disability* [online]. London: Alzheimer's Society. Available at: http://www.learningdisabilityanddementia.org/jennys-diary.html (accessed September 2018).

Watchman K. *Let's Talk about Death: A booklet about death and funerals for adults who have a learning disability* [online]. Available at: http://lx.iriss.org.uk/sites/default/files/resources/Let%27s%20talk%20about%20death.pdf (accessed September 2018).

Chapter 8: Eating and drinking

Chapter aim: to highlight the cognitive, environmental, physical and social issues that can affect the enjoyment of meal times for a person with a learning disability and dementia.

Everyone needs to eat and drink well to maintain good health, including people with dementia. However, they may find it increasingly difficult to eat and drink well, enjoy food and drink, and get pleasure from the social interaction associated with meal times. This is because:

- Sense of smell and taste will continually change as dementia progresses – food that was previously enjoyed can taste bland and be unappealing, so they may start to eat food they have not liked before or develop cravings for different, especially sweet, food.
- People may forget that they have just eaten, or save food to eat later.
- People may not recognise when they are feeling hungry or thirsty.
- People may forget what to do once food is in their mouth.
- Toothache or painful false teeth may prevent eating, although the person may not be able to explain this.
- It may be difficult to recognise cutlery and crockery or remember how to use them to eat and drink, even if they are thirsty or hungry.
- Hydration is as important as nutrition. If a person with dementia forgets to drink, it can affect the kidneys, bowel, skin and brain. Older people can lose up to two litres of fluid a day, which must be replaced. Watch out for gains and losses of weight as a result of a poor diet or poor hydration.

Help at meal times

People with dementia can be supported at meal times in the following ways:

- Reduce distracting noise levels at meal times and avoid speaking over a person to someone else.

- Only offer food and drink the person likes.
- Cut the food into small easily manageable pieces.
- If the person is not eating much, ensure that what they do eat is fresh and healthy and of maximum benefit to them.
- Try to find out how the person prefers to eat meals (e.g. sitting at a table or eating from a tray on their lap, alone or in a group).
- Ensure the person is sitting correctly to reduce the chance of choking, which is more likely to occur as the muscles used for swallowing become weaker.
- Try to find out if the person likes a drink with their meal or afterwards and what their preferred drink is.
- Sit and eat with the person to help provide cues and make the meal a more social opportunity.
- Use contrasting colour on the table – the plates should contrast with the table covering and, ideally, the food should contrast with the plate.
- Too much pattern can cause confusion and prevent the person enjoying meal times, as they may confuse the pattern with food.
- Use cutlery and cups that help the person to eat and drink. This will change depending on the stage of dementia.
- Describing what the food is, what it looks like and what it tastes like can help if the person is also visually impaired.
- If food needs to be blended, it is important to keep different types of food separate so that the different flavours can still be recognised even if the food looks different.
- Leave small snacks around (regularly replaced), perhaps along the route the person tends to walk regularly.

Chapter 8: Eating and drinking

The first table is visually confusing and it is hard to identify the crockery and cutlery on it, but the second table, using contrasting colours, makes things easy to identify.
A heavily patterned tablecloth can cause confusion and lead to the person with dementia trying to pick things off it.

Key point

New ways of supporting people at meal times will be needed to avoid dehydration and malnutrition. Try to maintain the person's involvement in the social aspects of meal times.

Links to Supporting Derek

1. Theresa and other carers need to check whether Derek is wearing the correct pair of glasses and that they are clean, to enable him to see the table and food clearly. If they are not, this will lead to an increase in his confusion.
2. The environment was very noisy, which proved distressing for Derek. He did not hear Theresa calling him to eat; he only saw her leaning over him, which he took as his cue to get up and go home to his mother.
3. The patterns on the tablecloth and carpet are complex and confusing.
4. Theresa became increasingly frustrated with Derek's behaviour and did not understand what he really needed in the following instances:
    - Derek did not respond to Theresa's request to go to the table because her instructions were complex and there was a lack of cues (e.g. looking at or smelling food).
    - Derek copied Peter by eating from his plate (modelling behaviour).

Activities

Activity 1

After checking for dietary requirements or allergies, take turns to offer someone else a biscuit, yoghurt, raisins, chocolate or similar food items. Consider:

1. What it feels like to 'be fed'.
2. Which consistency was easier to eat and why.

Activity 2

Consider, from Derek's perspective, why his lunch was such a confusing experience. Do any of these issues apply in your work place?

Activity 3

List the other local professionals who could be involved in providing additional support at meal times.
Who else should be involved and at what stage?

Further reading

Alzheimer's Society (2016) *Eating and Drinking, Factsheet 511LP* [online]. Available at: https://www.alzheimers.org.uk/get-support/daily-living/eating-drinking (accessed September 2018).

Dementia UK (2018) *Eating and Drinking for People with Dementia* [online]. Available at: https://www.dementiauk.org/understanding-dementia/advice-and-information-2/eating-and-drinking/ (accessed September 2018).

Tool 8B: Guidelines for helping people to eat well

- Make sure the environment is calm and quiet.
- Make sure there are regular intervals between meal times.
- Tables should not be set more than 30 minutes before eating.
- Meals should be served one course at a time.
- Finger food should be available if needed and regularly replaced.
- Staff should be present and involved at meal times.
- The same carer should stay with the person during a meal.
- Carers should not speak over the person who is being supported to eat.
- The correct glasses should be worn and they should be clean.
- Make sure the person is sitting upright and supported, to reduce the chance of choking.
- Small mouthfuls should be encouraged.
- Allow time for the person to swallow.
- Give clear verbal prompts.
- Offer the choice of a cup or mug, soft drink or water, tea or coffee.
- Help, but do not force.
- Sit at the person's eye level or just below, in front or slightly to the side.
- Use cutlery and cups that are adapted to the person's changing abilities.

Chapter 9: Night-time care

Chapter aim: to understand how sleep patterns are affected and to understand night-time waking as an opportunity for meaningful one-to-one interaction.

Even without dementia, people with a learning disability may have altered sleep patterns. This can be seen more often in people with autism, or some types of learning disability, such as Angelman syndrome, Down's syndrome and Prader Willi syndrome. If you are working with someone who has one of these conditions, it is worthwhile looking to see what kinds of sleep problems are associated with the condition.

Research has shown that supporting people who have sleep problems can also be one of the most difficult things for staff and families to cope with. Finding a way to manage a person's sleep problems can make a real difference to the stress levels of staff and families, and of course of the person with a learning disability and dementia themselves.

Sleep disruptions

Changes to night-time sleep caused by the onset of dementia can include:

- night terrors
- sleep talking
- sleep walking
- 'acting out' dreams
- enuresis (incontinence at night)
- night-time waking
- pain
- nocturnal seizures (as dementia progresses).

These are due to changes in the brain that can happen with dementia. Night-time changes can bring about sleepiness, poor co-ordination, short temper or aggression, poor memory during the day and even hallucinations, if sleep becomes very disrupted.

The body clock of a person with dementia can become increasingly disturbed and they will wake more often at night. However, they may not be aware that it is night time and may try to start their day by getting dressed or having breakfast, even if it is 4am.

Waking at night-time needs to be addressed for a range of reasons:

- To reduce the possibility of others being disturbed, if the person lives in shared accommodation.
- To avoid the use of excessive night-time sedation.
- To maintain the person in their own accommodation.
- To manage staff stress levels, and the effects that this in turn would have on residents.

Having finger food available at night, in areas where the person walks or sits, can help with nutrition.

Promoting sleep

A device such as a FitBit or similar can help to monitor sleep. This device is like a bracelet from which you can download information to a mobile phone, laptop or iPad: it monitors heart rate and pulse and can indicate how much uninterrupted sleep a person is getting at night. As with many other forms of technology, it may rely on the person having internet access to make best use of such devices.

Support at night-time can include:

- Reducing the person's anxiety if they think they are late or should be leaving to go somewhere.
- Being aware that disorientation at night-time might result from changes made to the environment during the day and decreased lighting and visibility.
- Determining if a need for the toilet or pain is preventing sleep.
- Talking quietly to the person rather than trying to get them straight back to bed – finding out whether something is worrying them, or what woke them may be helpful.
- Providing a hot drink (without caffeine) or something to eat.
- Staff wearing night-time clothing during the night can give the visual message to anyone who wakes that it is night-time. Seeing staff in their day clothes at 4am will wrongly suggest to the person with dementia that it is day time.
- Encouraging the person with dementia to go to bed when they are calm.

Consider your own actions at night-time; for example, try not to speak loudly, walk noisily, have music or the television turned on or carry out noisy household activities. Bright lights can indicate daylight and should be avoided.
Regular assessments of physical health should also identify any issues relating to pain and infection that may be affecting sleep. It may also be useful to consider melatonin, though this should be discussed with a psychiatrist prior to any use.

Key point

Waking at night is often a consequence of dementia. Staff responses and the environment can affect what happens when a person wakes. If a person with dementia wakes during the night and cannot be settled, consider providing them with a drink or snack or engaging them in a quiet activity.

Links to *Supporting Derek* film

We see Derek at lunchtime so we are not aware of his night-time routine. Towards the end of the film, when sitting comfortably on the sofa, he appears sleepy. There is an increased likelihood of night-time waking for Derek if he sleeps a lot during the day and does not get enough exercise.

Activities

Activity 1

Think about how you feel when your sleep pattern is disrupted? What time of day is the quietest in your house and provides you with time to yourself?

Activity 2

Think about the sleep pattern of a person you support. Consider how this affects their functioning and abilities the next day and why they may be more confused at certain times of day. For example, the person may wake from an afternoon nap and think it is morning.

Activity 3

If you work in a residential setting, consider the guidance available to staff providing support at night time. Does this need updating to accommodate the specific needs of people with a learning disability and dementia? If you do not have this guidance, or do not work in this type of setting, discuss what best practice in night time care may look like generally.

Further reading

Kerr D and Wilkinson H (2010) *Providing Good Care at Night for Older People: Practical approaches for use in nursing and care homes*. London: Jessica Kingsley Publishers.

Kerr D, Wilkinson H & Cunningham C (2008) *Supporting Older People in Care Homes at Night* [online]. Joseph Rowntree Foundation. Available at: https://www.jrf.org.uk/sites/default/files/jrf/migrated/files/night-care-older-people.pdf (accessed June 2018).

Chapter 9: Night-time care

Tool 9: Night-time waking – know the cycle

Too often we see the following night-time cycle:

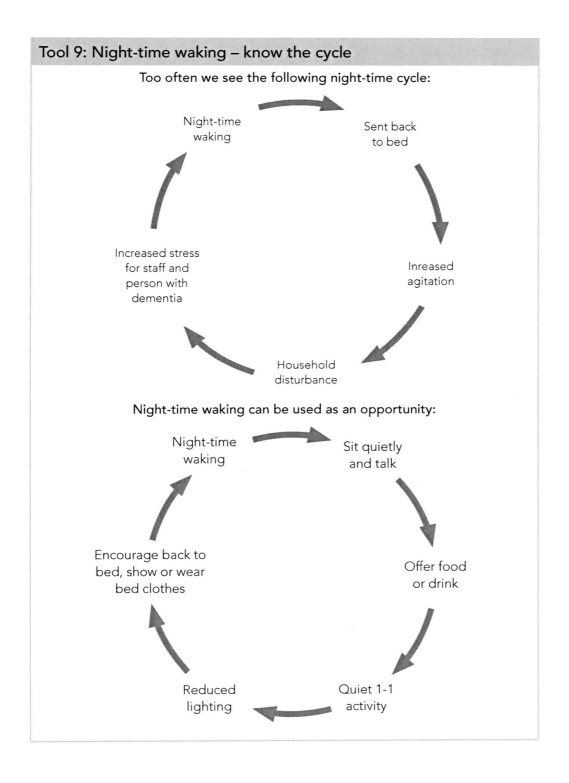

Night-time waking → Sent back to bed → Inreased agitation → Household disturbance → Increased stress for staff and person with dementia → Night-time waking

Night-time waking can be used as an opportunity:

Night-time waking → Sit quietly and talk → Offer food or drink → Quiet 1-1 activity → Reduced lighting → Encourage back to bed, show or wear bed clothes → Night-time waking

Chapter 10: Advanced dementia

Chapter aim: to raise awareness of the importance of a more holistic approach to providing care and support for people with a learning disability at an advanced stage of dementia.

Palliative care

Palliative care and end of life are often spoken about together. However, palliative care can, and often should, begin much earlier in the dementia process. Dementia will ultimately lead to death, usually from an associated condition, such as pneumonia, so it is important to think about what a 'good death' may involve and how a palliative approach can be introduced sooner.

A palliative approach means understanding of dying as part of a normal process. It brings together psychological and spiritual aspects of care with social and physical. Key areas include:

- pain relief
- making sure that we do not delay or hurry death
- providing support for the family
- maintaining a good quality of life.

People with a learning disability generally experience poorer health than people without a learning disability. Additionally, they have more complex needs and a higher degree of unmet medical needs. Yet ironically, people with a learning disability who are dying are less likely to access palliative care services, make use of complementary therapy or attend a hospice, even as a day patient.

End of life care

Communication difficulties and reduced capacity make decision-making and consent for medical treatment complicated. It is important that the person's wishes around their end of life care, location of care and funeral arrangements are known in the early stages of dementia. Indeed, many of these discussions now take place routinely with people who have a learning disability, just as they do among others without a learning disability. Plans for end of life care and funeral preferences are often routinely discussed as part of advanced care planning or when developing life-story work.

Many of us would like to choose where we die, and often home is the preferred option. This choice is not always offered to people with a learning disability, because there is a:

- lack of knowledge among staff and carers about the options that are available
- lack of knowledge about what the person wants, if they are unable to communicate this verbally
- lack of confidence among staff and carers about what a palliative care approach means
- need to meet the needs of other residents, if the person lives in shared accommodation
- lack of knowledge about end of life emotional and physical care issues
- fear about addressing end of life issues.

People with a learning disability and dementia are often not included in planning for their own end of life because they have not been told they have dementia, they do not know that they are dying or have an illness that will ultimately lead to their death. As we have seen, the person may not always understand their diagnosis. However, discussion can take place about the emotional and physical changes that are, and will, happen to enable end of life planning to take place.

Chapter 10: Advanced dementia

Derek does not appear to have had an explanation of the changes he is experiencing.

How to support and encourage a palliative care approach

- Know which professionals to involve at different stages. Regular visits from the GP can be helpful.

- Find out what the person knows about their condition and try to determine how much more information they would like.

- Ensure that pain relief is given routinely and not on request or 'as required' – the person may not be able to communicate when it is required.

- Offer the person a choice about where they would like to die. If they are living their family (most likely their parents or a sibling) ensure they know what help is available to enable the person to die at home.

- Make sure that there is access to hospice care in a location of the person's choice.

- Understand the person's cultural and religious beliefs around death and dying.

- Ensure that end of life care planning is given priority among care staff.

- Ensure that staff have support and training in end of life care issues and after the person they are supporting dies.
- Involve family and friends as appropriate right up to, and beyond, the end – they can often provide the most personal care and comfort.

You will notice that the key elements of end of life care of people with a learning disability are the same as for anyone else. However, there is often an assumption that something different is needed.

Involving a wide range of professionals in planning end of life care with people who have a learning disability at an earlier stage can remove some of this uncertainty.

Key point

Communication is key; communication with the person with a learning disability, their friends and family, staff and other professionals. It is necessary to think about 'when' a person with a learning disability and dementia will die, rather than 'if'. A palliative care approach should be in place sooner rather than later.

Links to *Supporting Derek* film

We are not given information about future planning that may have taken place with Derek. It may be possible to consider when and how this may happen in a training session.

Activities

Activity 1

Think about the stage at which a palliative care approach could be started. Consider the potential benefits and difficulties of beginning a palliative care approach at an earlier stage in dementia care for people with learning disabilities.

Activity 2

Consider how the experiences of palliative care in people with a learning disability compare with:

- palliative care with people who have illnesses other than dementia
- palliative care with people who do not have a learning disability.

Activity 3

List the professionals in your own area who will be involved as dementia progresses through to the terminal stage. If this is not known, the team can work together to produce this information.

Further reading

Alzheimer Scotland (2015) *Advanced Dementia Practice Model: Understanding and transforming advanced dementia and end of life care*. Edinburgh: Alzheimer Scotland. Available at: https://www.alzscot.org/campaigning/advanced_dementia_model (accessed September 2018).

European Association for Palliative Care (EAPC) Taskforce on People with Intellectual Disabilities (2016) *Defining Consensus Norms for Palliative Care of People with Intellectual Disabilities in Europe EAPC White Paper* [online]. Available at: https://www.ncbi.nlm.nih.gov/pubmed/26346181 (accessed September 2018).

McCallion, Hogan, Santos, McCarron, Service, Stemp Keller S, Fortea J, Bishop K, Watchman K, Janicki MP, Working Group of the International Summit on Intellectual Disability and Dementia (2017) Consensus statement of the International Summit on Intellectual Disability and Dementia related to end-of-life care in advanced dementia. *Journal of Applied Research in Intellectual Disabilities* **30** (6) 1160–1164.

Read S and Morris H (2008) *Living and Dying with Dignity: The best practice guide to end of life care for people with a learning disability* [online]. London: Mencap. Available at: https://www.bl.uk/collection-items/living-and-dying-with-dignity-the-best-practice-guide-to-endoflife-care-for-people-with-a-learning-disability (accessed September 2018).

Service KP, Watchman K, Hogan M, Janicki M, Berankova A & Cadovius N (2017) Dying well with an intellectual disability and dementia? *Journal of Dementia Care* **25** (4) 28–31.

Tuffrey-Wijne I & Watchman K (2015) Breaking bad news to people with learning disabilities and dementia. *Learning Disability Practice* **18** (7) 16–23.

Towers C (2017) *I'm Thinking Ahead* [online]. London: Together Matters and Foundation for People with Learning Disabilities. Available at: http://www.togethermatters.org.uk/im-thinking-ahead-pdf/ (accessed September 2018).

Chapter 10: Advanced dementia

Tool 10: Planning ahead

Use this tool to plan ahead for changing needs and end-of-life care. Put the person's name or photograph in the centre. In the surrounding circles, include the names of family, friends and professionals who will provide support and how they will do this. More circles can be added as needed.

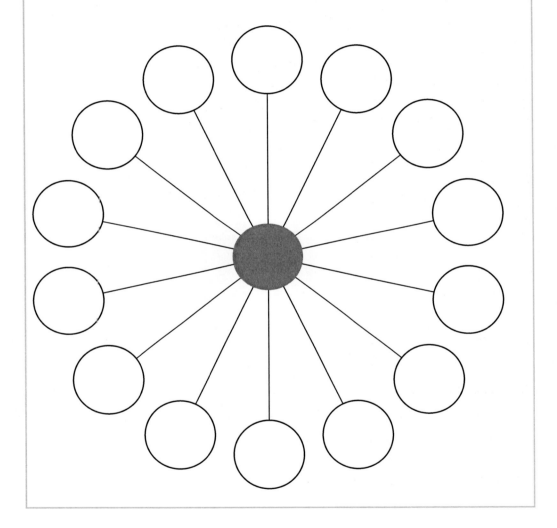

Additional resources

Capacity

The Adults with Incapacity Act (Scotland) 2000. Available at: http://www.opsi.gov.uk/legislation/scotland/acts2000/asp_20000004_en_1

The Mental Capacity Act (England & Wales) 2005. Available at: http://www.opsi.gov.uk/acts/acts2005/ukpga_20050009_en_1

Mental Capacity Act (Northern Ireland) 2016. Available at: http://www.legislation.gov.uk/nia/2016/18/contents/enacted

Websites

Alzheimer's Disease International: www.alz.co.uk and Alzheimer's Scotland: www.alzscot.org

Alzheimer's Society: www.alzheimers.org.uk

British Institute of Learning Disabilities: www.bild.org.uk

Down's Syndrome Association: www.downs-syndrome.org.uk

Down's Syndrome Scotland: www.dsscotland.org.uk

Dying Matters: www.dyingmatters.org

Enable: www.enable.org.uk

Foundation for People with Learning Disabilities: www.learningdisabilities.org.uk

Joseph Rowntree Foundation: www.jrf.org.uk

Learning Disability and Dementia (Karen Watchman's website): www.learningdisabilityanddementia.org

MacIntyre: https://www.macintyrecharity.org/our-work/supporting-people-with-dementia/

Mencap: www.mencap.org.uk

National Task Group on Intellectual disability and Dementia: http://aadmd.org/ntg

Palliative Care for People with Learning Disabilities: www.pcpld.org

Additional resources

PAMIS: www.dundee.ac.uk/pamis

RESPOND: www.respond.org.uk

Scottish Commission for Learning Disabilities: www.scld.org.uk

Social Care Institute for Excellence Dementia Gateway: https://www.scie.org.uk/dementia/living-with-dementia/learning-disabilities/